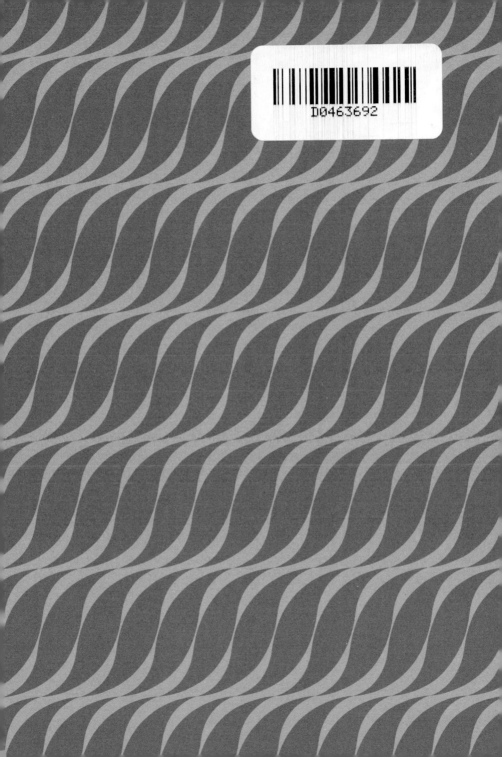

COOKING
FOR ONE

Consulting Editor:
Valerie Ferguson

southwater

Contents

Introduction

Mealtimes should be pleasant, relaxing occasions just as much for a person who lives alone as for a couple or a family. Life can be stressful and hectic, so enjoy some quality time for quality food and unwind over a favorite dish, attractively served and with the additional satisfaction of having cooked it yourself. The demands of a busy life may mean that this is not always possible, but even once a week it is worth it, not just for pleasure, but also, perhaps, to counterbalance a diet that can too easily become overloaded with take-out food and forzen dinners.

The recipes in this book have been devised for one person. There are ideas for all courses, ranging from substantial suppers to light lunches and snacks, as well as homemade soups, filling vegetarian main courses and melt-in-your-mouth desserts.

A helpful introduction offers advice on planning a healthy diet with the single person in mind, shopping for one, storing food and getting the most out of the microwave and freezer. Hints and tips throughout the book offer additional ideas and variations.

It is surprisingly easy to cook for one, and you can have exactly what you want for every meal!

Basic Nutrition

A healthy diet is one that is varied, so that all the four food groups, as well as essential vitamins and minerals, are included every day.

Starchy Foods

Bread, cereals, pasta, potatoes and rice provide complex carbohydrates, which fuel the body slowly, rather than with a sudden rush of sugar. This group, especially whole-grain foods, such as whole-wheat bread, is also an important source of dietary fiber.

Dairy Products

Milk, cheese, yogurt and butter provide protein, vitamins and minerals but may be very high in fats, particularly saturated fats, which are thought to raise cholesterol levels in the blood. Eat this group in moderation and consider switching to low-fat dairy products.

Proteins

Meat, fish, poultry, pulses, nuts and eggs supply many vitamins and

Above: Grains are the basis for a wide range of foods, all providing the starch we need for energy.

minerals as well as proteins, but some foods also have a high saturated fat content. Eat red meat in moderation. Fish, on the other hand, is often rich in polyunsaturated fats, which may lower levels of blood cholesterol. Skinning chicken before cooking removes almost all the fat. Pulses and nuts are an excellent source of many proteins. Eat eggs in moderation.

Vegetables & Fruit

Some authorities recommend eating five portions from this group each day, as they are thought to help prevent cancer. Raw fruit and vegetables are especially nutritious, providing carbohydrates, minerals and vitamins.

Buying & Storing Food

A well-stocked kitchen makes preparing meals easy, and the key is planning. Plan your menus for the next few days or even the week ahead, and make a shopping list that includes both fresh foods and staples that are running low or near to their use-by dates.

Perishable foods, such as butter, milk, cheese, meat and fish, should be stored in the refrigerator. Cover food or put it into rigid plastic containers. This preserves flavor and moisture and prevents odors of strong foods being transferred. Raw meat and poultry should be wrapped and placed where no drips can contaminate other food. Ripe fruits and perishable vegetables should be stored in the salad drawer. The temperature should be 35–40°F.

Root vegetables, such as carrots, potatoes and onions, are best stored in a cool, dark place, preferably in a rack where the air can circulate. Never store them in plastic, as they will rot.

The Freezer

A small freezer can be invaluable for storing both leftovers and fresh foods. Special offers in supermarkets often entail buying more than is needed for one meal, such as four chicken pieces. Either freeze three of them individually to be prepared on other occasions, or cook your favorite chicken dish and freeze three separate portions. Leftovers must be allowed to cool completely and then transferred to the freezer. Food should always be packed in rigid containers or wrapped in aluminum foil, two layers of plastic wrap or plastic freezer bags.

The Microwave

The microwave is a very economical way of cooking because it is so rapid, whereas heating an entire conventional oven for a single serving is rather extravagant. Always follow the manufacturer's instructions, including standing time, which is an integral part of cooking in the microwave. Never put anything metal in the microwave. Use microwave-proof containers, and do not cover dishes with aluminum foil. Most casseroles and stews, many soups and baked dishes cook well in the microwave.

The microwave is also ideal for defrosting frozen foods quickly, although not all are suitable. Again, follow the manufacturer's instructions and remember to remove any aluminum foil.

Above: Vegetables, especially raw, are rich in vitamins and fiber.

The Pantry

Stock this sensibly and you'll always have the wherewithal to make a tasty, satisfying meal. Begin with the basics and expand as you experiment, buying small amounts and keeping an eye on use-by dates.

Canned Vegetables & Pulses

Although fresh vegetables are best for most cooking, canned varieties are convenient, quick to use and usually available in small amounts. Popular and useful canned vegetables include artichoke hearts for livening up stir-fries, salads, risottos and pizzas, pimientos for flavoring stews and soups and corn for color and texture. Canned pulses are great time-savers, as they do not require soaking or prolonged cooking. Chickpeas, cannellini beans, green lentils, navy beans and red kidney beans all survive the canning process well. Rinse canned pulses in cold running water and drain well before use.

Above: A well-stocked pantry is an essential for the busy cook.

Cereals

Rice is a staple for over half the world and immensely useful. If you stock only one type, make it basmati, which has a superior flavor and fragrance. A mixture of basmati and wild rice works well. Dried pasta cooks in about 10 minutes and goes with almost everything, from vegetables to cheese and from meat to fish. Spaghetti and, perhaps, one pasta shape such as penne, will go with most sauces. It is well worth stocking some Chinese noodles to serve with stir-fries and other Chinese dishes.

Cooking & Salad Oils

Peanut oil is inexpensive and bland-tasting, so it will not mask delicate flavors. It is a good, all-purpose cooking oil, but you could also use vegetable or sunflower oil. Olive oil is good for most purposes, except deep-frying, and extra virgin olive oil is perfect for salad dressings. Other popular oils include sesame, used for flavoring Chinese and Asian dishes, and chili oil which adds instant and fiery spice to stir-fries and vegetables.

Herbs & Spices

Always buy dried herbs and spices in small amounts and keep well sealed, as they can get stale and flavorless very quickly. Useful basic dried herbs include bay leaves, marjoram or oregano, mint, rosemary and thyme. Some fresh herbs, such as cilantro, store best frozen in ice cube trays. Commercial pesto is a good substitute for fresh basil. One or two small pots of growing herbs, such as parsley and chives, add flavor to food and cheer up the kitchen. Useful basic spices include Chinese five-spice powder, coriander, cumin, nutmeg and turmeric. Freshly ground spices have more flavor, and freshly ground black pepper is a must.

Other Flavorings

If you like Chinese food, it is worth buying a bottle of good-quality soy sauce to flavor stir-fries. Tahini paste, made from sesame seeds, is useful for Middle Eastern dishes.

Tomatoes

Canned tomatoes are a multi-purpose pantry standby. Available whole or chopped, plain or with herbs, spices and other flavorings, they can be added to soups, stews, casseroles and pasta sauces. Tomato paste, a concentrated tomato sauce sold in tubes, cans and jars, imparts an instant tomato flavor to many dishes. A sun-dried version is also available. Passata is a thick sauce made from sieved tomatoes, also used to add a concentrated tomato flavor. Sun-dried tomatoes are available in bags or in jars of oil. The oil may be used in cooked dishes and salad dressings for a strong tomato flavor.

Above: A selection of oils, vinegars and flavorings to add interest to your dishes.

Fresh Tomato Soup

Served hot or chilled, this fresh-tasting soup is easy to prepare.

Serves 1

INGREDIENTS
9 ounces ripe tomatoes
¼ cup chicken or vegetable stock
1½ teaspoons sun-dried tomato paste
1–1½ teaspoons balsamic vinegar
pinch of sugar
1 teaspoon fresh basil leaves
salt and freshly ground black pepper
fresh basil leaves, to garnish
toasted cheese croûtes and crème fraîche,
  to serve

1 Plunge the tomatoes into boiling water for 30 seconds, then refresh in cold water. Peel off the skins and quarter the tomatoes. Put them in a large saucepan and pour in the chicken or vegetable stock.

2 Bring to a boil, reduce the heat, cover and simmer for 10 minutes, until the tomatoes are pulpy.

3 Stir in the tomato paste, vinegar, sugar and basil. Season with salt and pepper, then cook gently, stirring, for another 2 minutes.

4 Process the soup in a blender or food processor, then return to the pan and reheat gently. Serve topped with one or two toasted cheese croûtes and a spoonful of crème fraîche, garnished with basil leaves.

COOK'S TIP: To make cheese croûtes, toast slices of French bread sprinkled with Parmesan.

Thai-style Chicken Soup

Coconut milk, lemongrass, ginger and lime make a fragrant soup.

Serves 1

INGREDIENTS
1 teaspoon vegetable oil
1 small fresh red chile, seeded and chopped
1 garlic clove, crushed
1 small leek, thinly sliced
⅔ cup chicken stock
7 tablespoons coconut milk
1–2 boneless, skinless chicken thighs, cut
   into bite-size pieces
1½ teaspoons Thai fish sauce
½ lemongrass stalk
¼ teaspoon finely chopped fresh ginger root
pinch of sugar
1 kaffir lime leaf (optional)
¼ cup frozen peas, thawed
2 teaspoons chopped cilantro

1 Heat the oil in a large saucepan and cook the chile and garlic for about 2 minutes. Add the leek and cook for another 2 minutes.

2 Stir in the chicken stock and coconut milk and bring to a boil over medium heat.

3 Add the chicken, with the fish sauce, lemongrass, ginger, sugar and lime leaf, if using. Simmer, covered, for 15 minutes or until the chicken is tender, stirring occasionally.

4 Add the peas and cook for another 3 minutes. Remove the lemongrass. Stir in the cilantro before serving.

Zucchini Soup with Small Pasta Shapes

The pasta makes this quite a substantial soup which, served with crusty bread and cheese, would make a meal in itself.

Serves 1

INGREDIENTS
1 tablespoon olive or
   sunflower oil
1 small onion, finely chopped
1½ cups chicken stock
8 ounces zucchini
¼ cup small soup pasta
lemon juice
salt and freshly ground
   black pepper
2 teaspoons chopped
   fresh chervil
sour cream, to garnish

2 Meanwhile, grate the zucchini and stir into the boiling stock with the pasta. Turn down the heat and simmer for 10 minutes, until the pasta is tender. Season to taste with lemon juice, salt and pepper.

3 Stir in the chervil and add a swirl of sour cream before serving.

VARIATION: This attractive, summery soup can be made with cucumber if zucchini are unavailable. In this case, use chopped fennel, tarragon or dill instead of chervil.

1 Heat the oil in a large saucepan and add the onion. Cover and cook gently for about 20 minutes, until very soft but not colored, stirring occasionally. Add the stock and bring to a boil.

COOK'S TIP: If you don't have any fresh stock, use good-quality canned chicken or beef consommé instead of a bouillon cube.

Mussels Steamed in White Wine

This classic French dish is simple to prepare. Serve with plenty of crusty French bread to mop up the juices.

Serves 1

INGREDIENTS
1¼ pounds fresh mussels
5 tablespoons dry
   white wine
1 large shallot, finely chopped
bouquet garni
freshly ground
   black pepper

1 Discard any broken mussels and those with open shells that refuse to close when tapped. Under cold running water, scrape the mussel shells with a knife to remove any barnacles and pull out the stringy "beards." Soak the mussels in several changes of cold water for at least 1 hour.

COOK'S TIP: For Mussels with Cream Sauce, cook as above, but transfer the mussels to a warmed bowl and cover to keep warm. Strain the cooking liquid through a muslin-lined sieve into a large saucepan and boil for 7–10 minutes to reduce by half. Stir in 4 teaspoons whipping cream and 1½ teaspoons chopped parsley, then add the mussels. Cook for about 1 more minute to reheat the mussels.

2 In a heavy flameproof casserole, combine the wine, shallot, bouquet garni and plenty of pepper. Bring to a boil over medium-high heat and cook for 2 minutes.

3 Add the mussels and cook, tightly covered, for 5 minutes, or until the mussels open, shaking and tossing the pan occasionally. Discard any mussels that do not open.

4 Using a slotted spoon, transfer the mussels to a warmed soup plate. Tilt the casserole a little and hold for a few seconds to let any sand settle in the bottom. Spoon or pour the cooking liquid onto the mussels, then serve immediately with crusty French bread.

VARIATION: Instead of white wine, use the same amount of dry cider. If you prefer a thicker sauce, stir an egg yolk into the cooking liquid before pouring it over the mussels.

Marinated Mixed Vegetables with Basil Oil

Basil oil is a must for drizzling onto plain stir-fried vegetables. It will keep in the refrigerator for up to two weeks.

Serves 1

INGREDIENTS
1½ teaspoons olive oil
1 garlic clove, crushed
zest of ½ lemon, finely grated
7-ounce can artichoke
    hearts, drained
1 large leek, sliced
4 ounces patty pan squash,
    halved, if large
1 large plum tomato, cut into
    segments lengthwise
½ ounce fresh basil leaves
⅔ cup extra virgin
    olive oil
salt and freshly ground
    black pepper

2 Place the artichokes, leek, patty pan squash and plum tomato in a large bowl, pour in the marinade and set aside for 30 minutes.

3 Meanwhile, make the basil oil. Blend the fresh basil leaves with the extra virgin olive oil in a food processor until puréed, pushing down a couple of times with a spatula.

1 Thoroughly combine the olive oil, garlic and lemon zest in a bowl, to make a marinade.

4 Heat a wok, then stir-fry the marinated vegetables for 3–4 minutes, tossing well. Drizzle basil oil on the vegetables and serve.

Chicken Liver & Bacon Salad

Warm salads, with their interesting combination of hot and cold elements, are becoming increasingly popular.

Serves 1

INGREDIENTS

2 ounces young spinach,
  stems removed
¼ frisée lettuce
2 tablespoons peanut or
  sunflower oil
1–2 thick slices bacon,
  cut into strips
1 slice day-old bread, crusts removed and
  cut into short fingers
4 ounces chicken livers
5 cherry tomatoes
salt and freshly ground
  black pepper

1 Place the salad leaves in a bowl. Heat half the oil in a large frying pan. Add the bacon and cook for 3–4 minutes or until crisp and brown. Remove with a slotted spoon and drain on paper towels.

2 To make the croutons, fry the bread in the bacon-flavored oil until crisp and golden. Drain on paper towels.

3 Heat the remaining oil, add the chicken livers and cook briskly for 2–3 minutes. Place the livers on the salad leaves, and add the bacon, croutons and tomatoes. Season, toss and serve.

Pear with Stilton

This is a classic British appetizer, but it also makes an easy and filling snack at any time of day.

Serves 1

INGREDIENTS
1 ripe pear, lightly chilled
1 ounce Stilton cheese
1 tablespoon cottage cheese
freshly ground
　black pepper
watercress sprigs, to garnish

FOR THE DRESSING
1 tablespoon olive oil
1 teaspoon lemon juice
1½ teaspoons toasted
　poppy seeds
salt and freshly ground
　black pepper

1 First make the dressing: place the olive oil, lemon juice, poppy seeds and seasoning in a screw-topped jar and shake together until emulsified.

2 Cut the pear in half lengthwise, then scoop out the core and cut out the calyx from the rounded end.

3 Beat together the Stilton, cottage cheese and a little pepper. Divide this mixture evenly between the cavities in the pear halves.

4 Shake the dressing to mix it again, then spoon it onto the pear. Serve garnished with watercress.

Salmon with Yogurt & Mint Dressing

Salmon is a very rich fish and is delicious, broiled and served with this light and delicate sauce.

Serves 1

INGREDIENTS
4-inch piece cucumber
6 fresh mint leaves
⅔ cup plain yogurt
6 ounces salmon fillet, scaled
olive oil, for brushing
salt and freshly ground black pepper
mint sprigs, to garnish
fresh spinach leaves,
    to serve

3 Chop the mint leaves. Place the chopped mint leaves in a bowl with the yogurt.

1 Peel the cucumber, slice in half lengthwise and remove the seeds.

2 Grate the cucumber into a sieve, salt lightly and drain for about 5 minutes.

4 Squeeze out any excess juice from the cucumber and stir into the bowl with the yogurt and mint. Season with black pepper and set aside. Preheat the broiler until medium hot.

COOK'S TIP: Cover and store any leftover yogurt and mint dressing in the refrigerator. You can serve it with plain lamb chops the following day.

5 Brush the salmon with olive oil and season with a little salt. Broil for 3 minutes, skin-side up, then carefully turn it over and broil for about 2 minutes on the other side. The skin should be browned and crisp.

6 Serve on a bed of spinach with the yogurt and cucumber dressing. Garnish with mint and sprinkle on some freshly ground black pepper.

Smoked Haddock Fillet with Quick Parsley Sauce

Make any herb sauce with this method, making sure it is thickened and seasoned well to complement the smoky flavor of the fish.

Serves 1

INGREDIENTS
8 ounces smoked haddock fillet
2 tablespoons butter, softened
2 tablespoons all-purpose flour
⅔ cup milk
1–2 tablespoons chopped fresh parsley, plus extra, to garnish
salt and freshly ground black pepper

1 Smear the fish fillet on both sides with half the butter and preheat the broiler until medium-hot.

2 Beat the remaining butter and flour together in a bowl to make a paste.

3 Broil the fish for 10–15 minutes, turning when necessary. Meanwhile, heat the milk until just below the boiling point. Add the flour mixture in small pats, whisking constantly over the heat. Continue until the sauce is smooth and thick.

4 Stir in the seasoning and parsley and serve poured onto the fish garnished with parsley.

Tuna with Cilantro Crust & Mango Salsa

Fresh tuna is very meaty and filling and is perfectly matched with a fruity salsa that takes only moments to make.

Serves 1

INGREDIENTS
finely grated zest of ¼ lemon
¼ teaspoon black peppercorns
1 tablespoon finely
    chopped onion
1½ teaspoons chopped cilantro
6 ounces fresh tuna steak
2 tablespoons olive oil

FOR THE SALSA
¼ mango, peeled and diced
1 tablespoon lime juice
1 teaspoon grated lime zest
¼ red chile, seeded and
    finely chopped

1 First, make the salsa. Mix the mango, lime juice, zest and chile in a bowl and marinate for at least 1 hour.

2 Combine the lemon zest, black peppercorns, onion and cilantro in a coffee grinder to make a coarse paste.

3 Spread this on one side of the steak with the flat side of a knife.

4 Heat the olive oil in a heavy frying pan until it begins to smoke. Add the tuna, paste-side down, and fry until a crust forms. Lower the heat and turn the steak to cook for one minute. Pat off excess oil with paper towels. Serve with mango salsa.

Red Snapper with Herb Salsa

This simple dish is delicious served with mixed salad leaves, garnished with cilantro and curls of orange zest.

Serves 1

INGREDIENTS
6 ounces snapper fillet
1 teaspoon vegetable oil
¼ ounce butter
salt and freshly ground black pepper

FOR THE SALSA
½ ounce cilantro or parsley leaves
¼ cup olive oil
1 garlic clove, chopped
1 small tomato, cored and chopped
1½ teaspoons fresh orange juice
1 teaspoon sherry vinegar
pinch of salt

2 Transfer to a bowl. Stir in the orange juice, vinegar and salt. Set the salsa aside. Rinse the fish and pat dry. Sprinkle with salt and pepper.

3 Heat the oil and butter in a large nonstick frying pan. When hot, add the fish and cook for 2-3 minutes, until the flesh is opaque.

1 First make the salsa. Place the cilantro or parsley, oil and garlic in a food processor or blender. Process until almost smooth. Add the tomato and pulse on and off several times; the mixture should be slightly chunky.

4 Carefully transfer the fish to a warmed dinner plate using a spatula. Top with a spoonful of salsa. Serve additional salsa on the side.

Flounder & Pesto Parcel

Wrapping the fish in a parcel helps keep it moist during cooking.

Serves 1

INGREDIENTS
2 tablespoons butter
1 teaspoon pesto sauce
2 small flounder fillets
¼ small fennel bulb, cut into matchsticks
1 small carrot, cut into matchsticks
1 small zucchini, cut into matchsticks
½ teaspoon finely grated lemon zest
sunflower oil, for brushing
salt and freshly ground black pepper
fresh basil leaves, to garnish

1 Preheat the oven to 375°F. Beat half the butter with the pesto and seasoning to taste. Skin the fillets, then spread the pesto butter on the skinned-side and roll up, starting from the thick end.

2 Melt the remaining butter in a pan. Add the fennel and carrot and sauté for 3 minutes. Add the zucchini and cook for 2 minutes. Remove from heat. Add the lemon zest and season.

3 Oil a square of waxed paper. Spoon the vegetables into the center, then place the rolls on top. Seal the parcel and place in a roasting pan. Bake for 15–20 minutes. Open up the parcel and sprinkle with the basil.

Skate with Lemon

Lemon and capers are classic partners for fish.

Serves 1

INGREDIENTS
1 small skate wing, about 6–8 ounces
seasoned flour
4½ teaspoons olive oil
1 garlic clove, crushed
1 teaspoon finely grated lemon zest
2 tablespoons lemon juice
1½ teaspoons capers, rinsed, drained
  and chopped
1½ teaspoons chopped fresh flat-leaf parsley
1 teaspoon chopped fresh basil
1 teaspoon snipped fresh chives
salt and freshly ground black pepper

1 Lightly dust the skate in the seasoned flour. Heat 1½ teaspoons of the oil in a large frying pan and, when hot, add the skate and fry for 8–10 minutes, turning once.

2 Meanwhile, combine the remaining oil, the garlic, lemon zest and juice in a bowl with the capers, parsley, basil, chives and seasoning.

3 Pour the sauce into a pan to warm through. Serve the skate with the sauce spooned on top.

Right: Flounder & Pesto Parcel (top); Skate with Lemon

Mediterranean Shrimp

Skewered shrimp make a delicious summer supper dish.

Serves 1

INGREDIENTS
4 raw jumbo shrimp, peeled
1 garlic clove, finely chopped
4 teaspoons finely chopped fresh parsley
1 small fresh rosemary sprig, leaves removed
   and finely chopped
pinch of dried chile flakes
3 tablespoons fresh lime juice
1½ teaspoons olive oil
salt and freshly ground black pepper
green salad, to serve

1 Remove the black thread that runs along the back of the shrimp. Make cuts along the back, without cutting through, then carefully fan out.

2 Blend the garlic, herbs, chile flakes, lime juice, oil and seasoning in a bowl. Add the shrimp, stir well and marinate for 1 hour. Soak four wooden skewers in warm water for at least 30 minutes.

3 Preheat the broiler until very hot. Thread two shrimp onto each pair of skewers and broil for 2–3 minutes. Remove the shrimp from the skewers and serve with green salad.

Right: Mediterranean Shrimp (top); Scallops with Lemon & Thyme

Scallops with Lemon & Thyme

If using the shell, make sure it is well scrubbed first.

Serves 1

INGREDIENTS
1 tablespoon olive oil
1 garlic clove, finely chopped
leaves from 1 fresh thyme sprig
1 small bay leaf
1 teaspoon chopped fresh parsley
4 fresh scallops, rinsed
½ small shallot, finely chopped
1 teaspoon balsamic vinegar
1½ teaspoons lemon juice
2 tablespoons chicken or vegetable stock
salt and freshly ground
   black pepper
6 baby spinach leaves, to garnish

1 Blend the olive oil, garlic, thyme, bay leaf and parsley in a bowl. Add the scallops and marinate for 1 hour. Heat a heavy frying pan. Remove the scallops from the marinade and sear for about 30 seconds on each side. Transfer to a plate and keep warm.

2 Add the marinade to the pan with the shallot, balsamic vinegar, lemon juice and stock. Cook over high heat for 2–3 minutes, until the stock is well reduced. Discard the bay leaf and season. Arrange the spinach leaves on a serving plate, place the scallops in the shell and pour on the juices.

Chicken with Tomatoes & Olives

Chicken breasts or turkey, veal or pork cutlets may be flattened for quick and even cooking.

Serves 1

INGREDIENTS
5–6 ounces skinless, boneless
    chicken breast
pinch of cayenne pepper
4½ teaspoons extra virgin
    olive oil
1 garlic clove,
    finely chopped
10 black olives
2 plum tomatoes, chopped
1 tablespoon fresh basil leaves
salt

1 Carefully remove the fillet (the long finger-shaped muscle on the back of the breast) and reserve for another use.

2 Place the chicken breast between two sheets of waxed paper or plastic wrap and pound with the flat-side of a meat mallet or roll out with a rolling pin to flatten to about ½ inch thick. Season with salt and cayenne pepper.

COOK'S TIP: If the tomato skins are tough, remove them by scoring the base of each tomato with a knife, then plunging them into boiling water for 30 seconds. The skin should simply peel off.

3 Heat 1 tablespoon of the olive oil in a large frying pan over medium-high heat. Add the chicken and cook for 4–5 minutes, until golden brown and just cooked, turning it once. Transfer the chicken to a warmed serving plate and keep warm.

4 Wipe out the frying pan and return to the heat. Add the remaining olive oil and fry the garlic for 1 minute, until golden and fragrant. Stir in the olives, cook for another 1 minute, then stir in the tomatoes.

5 Shred the basil leaves and stir into the olive and tomato mixture, then spoon it onto the chicken and serve.

Chicken & Cilantro with Snowpeas

Stir-fries are probably the original fast food, taking only minutes to cook and tasting utterly wonderful.

Serves 1

INGREDIENTS
1 skinless, boneless chicken breast
2 ounces snowpeas
1 tablespoon vegetable oil, plus extra for
    deep-frying
1 garlic clove, finely chopped
1 teaspoon grated fresh ginger root
2 scallions, cut into
    1½-inch lengths
½ teaspoon sesame oil
1 tablespoon chopped cilantro
boiled rice, to serve

FOR THE MARINADE
¼ teaspoon cornstarch
1 teaspoon light soy sauce
1 teaspoon medium dry sherry
1 teaspoon vegetable oil

FOR THE SAUCE
¼ teaspoon cornstarch
1 teaspoon dark soy sauce
2 tablespoons chicken stock
1 teaspoon oyster sauce

1 Cut the chicken into strips about ½ x 1½ inches. To make the marinade, blend together the cornstarch and soy sauce. Stir in the sherry and oil. Pour onto the chicken pieces, and let sit for 30 minutes.

2 Trim the snowpeas and plunge into a pan of boiling salted water. Bring back to a boil, then drain and refresh them under cold running water. Drain again.

3 To make the sauce, combine the cornstarch, soy sauce, stock and oyster sauce and set aside.

4 Heat the oil in a deep-fryer. Drain the chicken strips and fry for about 30 seconds to brown. Drain and transfer to a plate, with a slotted spoon.

5 Heat half the vegetable oil in a preheated wok and add the garlic and ginger. Stir-fry for 30 seconds. Add the snowpeas and stir-fry for another 1–2 minutes. Transfer to a plate and keep warm.

6 Heat the remaining vegetable oil in the wok, add the scallions and stir-fry for 1–2 minutes. Add the chicken and stir-fry for 2 minutes. Pour in the sauce, reduce the heat and cook until it thickens and the chicken is cooked through.

7 Stir in the sesame oil and chopped cilantro, and pour the mixture over the snowpeas. Serve with fresh boiled rice.

Duck Breast with Pineapple & Ginger

Boneless duck breast is available at most supermarkets and makes a substantial meal for one.

Serves 1

INGREDIENTS
1 boneless duck breast
2 scallions, chopped
1½ teaspoons light soy sauce
4-ounce can pineapple rings
4 teaspoons water
1 piece drained Chinese crystallized ginger
   in syrup, plus 2 teaspoons syrup from
   the jar
1½ teaspoons cornstarch, mixed into a thin
   paste with a little water
salt and freshly ground black pepper
egg noodles, baby spinach and
   green beans, to serve
1 tablespoon strips green bell pepper,
   to garnish
1 tablespoon strips red bell pepper, to garnish

1 Carefully remove the skin from the duck breast. Select a shallow bowl that will fit into your steamer and that will accommodate the duck breast. Spread out the chopped scallions in the bowl, arrange the duck breast on top and cover with nonstick baking paper.

2 Set the steamer over boiling water and cook the duck breast for 1 hour or until it is tender. Remove the duck breast from the steamer and set aside until it is cool enough to handle.

3 Cut the duck into thin slices. Place on a plate and moisten with a little of the cooking juices from the steaming bowl. Strain the remaining juices into a saucepan with the soy sauce and set aside. Cover the duck slices with the baking paper or foil and keep warm.

4 Drain the canned pineapple rings, reserving 1 tablespoon of the juice. Add this to the reserved cooking juices in the pan, together with the measured water. Stir in the ginger syrup, then stir in the cornstarch paste and cook, stirring, until thickened. Season to taste.

5 Cut the pineapple and ginger into attractive shapes. Put the cooked noodles, baby spinach and green beans on a plate, add slices of duck and top with the pineapple, ginger and pepper strips. Pour on the sauce and serve.

Braised Ham with Madeira Sauce

With very little effort or expense, you can transform an unexciting ham steak into an elegant gourmet dish.

Serves 1

INGREDIENTS
2 tablespoons unsalted butter
1 shallot, finely chopped
1½ teaspoons all-purpose flour
1 teaspoon tomato paste
¼ cup beef stock
4½ teaspoons Madeira
6–7 ounces ham steak
salt and freshly ground black pepper
watercress, to garnish
creamed potatoes, to serve

1 Melt half the butter in a heavy, medium-size saucepan over medium-high heat, then add the shallot and cook for 2–3 minutes, until just softened, stirring frequently.

COOK'S TIP: To make the sauce a deeper color, add a few drops of gravy juice to the stock.

2 Sprinkle on the flour and cook for 3–4 minutes, until well browned, stirring constantly, then whisk in the tomato paste and stock and season with pepper. Simmer over low heat until the sauce is reduced by about half, stirring occasionally.

3 Taste the sauce and adjust the seasoning, then stir in the Madeira and cook for 2–3 minutes.

4 Strain into a small bowl and keep warm in a low oven or over a saucepan of just simmering water.

5 Snip the edges of the ham steak to prevent it from curling. Melt the remaining butter in a frying pan over medium-high heat, then add the ham steak and cook for 4–5 minutes or until cooked through, turning once. Transfer the ham to a warmed plate and pour on the sauce. Garnish with watercress and serve with creamed potatoes.

Lamb Chops with Mint

The classic combination is here given a slightly unusual twist.

Serves 1

INGREDIENTS
2 loin lamb chops or 1 double loin
    lamb chop, about ¾-inch thick
coarsely ground black pepper
fresh mint, to garnish
sautéed potatoes, to serve

FOR THE MINT VINAIGRETTE
1½ teaspoons white wine vinegar
¼ teaspoon honey
1 small garlic clove, very
    finely chopped
1 tablespoon extra virgin
    olive oil
1 tablespoon finely chopped
    fresh mint
1 small tomato, peeled, seeded and
    finely diced
salt and freshly ground black pepper

1 First, make the vinaigrette. Put the vinegar, honey, garlic, salt and pepper in a small bowl and whisk thoroughly to combine. Slowly whisk in the oil, then stir in the mint and tomato and set aside for up to 1 hour.

2 Put the lamb chops on a board and trim off any excess fat. Sprinkle with the pepper and press onto both sides of the meat, coating it evenly.

3 Lightly oil a cast iron griddle and set over high heat until very hot, but not smoking. Place the chops on the griddle and reduce the heat to medium. Cook the chops for 6–7 minutes, turning once, or until done as desired. Serve the chops with the vinaigrette and the sautéed potatoes, garnished with mint.

Peppered Steak in Beer

Robust flavors for a hearty appetite. Serve with salad and baked potatoes.

Serves 1

INGREDIENTS
6 ounces beef sirloin or rump steak,
   about 1-inch thick
1 garlic clove, crushed
2 tablespoons brown ale or stout
1½ teaspoons dark brown sugar
1½ teaspoons Worcestershire sauce
1 teaspoon corn oil
1 teaspoon crushed black peppercorns

1 Place the steak in a deep dish and add the garlic, ale or stout, sugar, Worcestershire sauce and oil. Turn to coat evenly in the marinade, and then let marinate in the refrigerator for 2–3 hours or overnight.

2 Remove the steak from the dish and reserve the marinade. Sprinkle the peppercorns onto the steak and press them into the surface. Preheat the broiler.

3 Cook the steak under a hot broiler, basting it occasionally with the reserved marinade during cooking.

4 Turn the steak once during cooking and cook it for 3–6 minutes on each side, depending on how rare you like it.

COOK'S TIP: Take care when basting with the marinade; spoon on just a small amount at a time.

Chili Beef with Basil

This is a dish for chili lovers! It is very easy to prepare and cook.

Serves 1

INGREDIENTS
about 3 tablespoons peanut oil
8–10 large fresh basil leaves
5 ounces rump steak
1 tablespoon Thai fish sauce
½ teaspoon dark brown sugar
1 fresh red chile, sliced into rings
1 garlic clove, chopped
½ teaspoon chopped fresh
   ginger root
1 small shallot, thinly sliced
1 tablespoon chopped fresh
   basil leaves
dash of lemon juice
salt and freshly ground
   black pepper
boiled rice, to serve

2 Cut the steak across the grain into thin strips. In a bowl, combine the fish sauce and sugar. Add the beef, mix well, then let marinate for about 30 minutes.

3 Reheat the oil until hot, add the chile, garlic, ginger and shallot and stir-fry for 30 seconds. Add the beef and chopped basil, then stir-fry for about 3 minutes. Flavor with lemon juice and add seasoning to taste.

COOK'S TIP: To reduce the heat of the chile, remove the seeds before cooking. Wash your hands carefully after handling cut chiles.

1 Heat the oil in a preheated wok and, when hot, add the whole basil leaves and fry for about 1 minute, until crisp. Drain on paper towels. Remove the wok from heat and pour off all but 1 tablespoon of the oil.

4 Transfer to a warmed serving plate, sprinkle on the fried basil leaves and serve immediately with boiled rice.

Red Bell Pepper Stuffed with Ground Beef

This easy all-in-one dish may be cooked in a conventional oven or, for speed and economy, in the microwave.

Serves 1

INGREDIENTS
1 red bell pepper
½ small onion
1 celery stalk
1 cup ground beef
1 tablespoon olive oil
2–3 button mushrooms
pinch of ground cinnamon
salt and freshly ground
    black pepper
flat-leaf parsley, to garnish
green salad, to serve

1 Cut the top off the red pepper and reserve it. Remove the seeds and membranes from the pepper.

2 Finely chop the onion and celery. Set aside. Sauté the ground beef in a nonstick frying pan for a few minutes, stirring until it is no longer red. Transfer to a plate.

3 Pour half the oil into the frying pan and sauté the chopped vegetables over high heat until the onion starts to brown. Add the mushrooms and stir in the partly cooked beef. Season with the cinnamon, salt and pepper. Cook over low heat for 15 minutes.

4 Preheat the oven to 375°F. Cut a sliver off the base of the pepper so it stands level, spoon in the beef mixture, and replace the lid. Place in an oiled dish, drizzle on the remaining oil and cook for 20 minutes. Garnish with parsley. Serve with green salad.

VARIATION: You could use ground lamb for this dish instead of beef, if you prefer.

Stir-fried Vegetables with Cashews

This versatile stir-fry will accommodate most other combinations of vegetables—you do not have to use the selection suggested here.

Serves 1

INGREDIENTS
1 small carrot
½ small red bell pepper, seeded
½ small green bell pepper, seeded
1 small zucchini
1 ounce green beans
1–2 scallions
1 teaspoon extra virgin olive oil
1 curry leaf
pinch of white cumin seeds
1 dried red chile
1 tablespoon cashews
pinch of salt
1½ teaspoons lemon juice
fresh mint leaves,
    to garnish

1 Prepare the vegetables: cut the carrot, peppers and zucchini into matchsticks, halve the beans and chop the scallions. Set aside.

2 Heat the oil in a nonstick wok or frying pan and fry the curry leaf, cumin seeds and dried chile for about 1 minute.

3 Add the vegetables and nuts and stir them around gently. Add the salt and lemon juice. Continue to stir and cook for 3–5 minutes.

4 Transfer to a serving dish, garnish with mint leaves and serve.

COOK'S TIP: If you are very short on time, use frozen mixed vegetables, which also work well in this dish.

Herbed Wild Rice Pilaf

A nutritious one-pot meal.

Serves 1

INGREDIENTS
⅓ cup mixed brown basmati
    and wild rice
1 teaspoon olive oil
½ small onion, chopped
1 garlic clove, crushed
½ teaspoon ground cumin
½ teaspoon ground turmeric
2 tablespoons golden raisins
¾ cup vegetable stock
1 tablespoon chopped fresh mixed herbs
salt and freshly ground black pepper
fresh herb sprigs and 1 tablespoon pistachios,
    to garnish

1 Wash the rice in a sieve under cold running water, then drain well. Heat the oil in a saucepan, add the onion and garlic and cook gently for 5 minutes, stirring occasionally.

2 Add the spices and rice and cook gently for 1 minute, stirring. Stir in the golden raisins and stock, bring to a boil, cover and simmer for 20–25 minutes, until almost all the liquid has been absorbed, stirring occasionally.

3 Stir in the chopped herbs and season to taste with salt and pepper. Spoon the pilaf into a warmed bowl and garnish with herb sprigs and pistachios.

Roast Baby Vegetables

Serve with black olives, if desired.

Serves 1

INGREDIENTS
5½ ounces mixed baby vegetables, such as
    eggplant, onion or shallot, zucchini, corn
    and button mushrooms
½ small red bell pepper, seeded and cut into
    large pieces
1 garlic clove, finely chopped
1 teaspoon olive oil
1 teaspoon chopped fresh mixed herbs
2–3 cherry tomatoes
¼ cup coarsely grated mozzarella cheese
salt and freshly ground black pepper
black olives, to serve (optional)

1 Preheat the oven to 425°F. Cut all the mixed baby vegetables in half lengthwise.

2 Place the baby vegetables and pepper in a dish with the garlic and seasoning. Drizzle on the oil and toss the vegetables to coat them. Bake for 20 minutes, stirring once.

3 Remove the dish from the oven and stir in the herbs. Add the tomatoes and top with the mozzarella. Bake for 5–10 more minutes.

Right: Herbed Wild Rice Pilaf (top);
Roast Baby Vegetables

Thai Noodles with Chinese Chives

This recipe requires a little time for preparation, but everything is cooked speedily in a hot wok and should be eaten immediately.

Serves 1

INGREDIENTS
3 ounces dried rice noodles
¼ teaspoon grated fresh ginger root
1½ teaspoons light soy sauce
2½ teaspoons vegetable oil
2 ounces Quorn or tempeh, cut into
    small cubes
1 garlic clove, crushed
1 small onion, cut into thin wedges
1 ounce fried tofu, thinly sliced
1 small green chile, seeded and finely sliced
2 ounces bean sprouts
1 ounce Chinese chives, cut into 2-inch
    lengths
2 tablespoons roasted peanuts,
    coarsely ground
1½ teaspoons dark soy sauce
1½ teaspoons chopped cilantro

1 Place the noodles in a bowl, cover with warm water and soak for 20–30 minutes, then drain. Blend together the ginger, light soy sauce and 1 teaspoon of the oil in a bowl. Stir in the Quorn or tempeh and set aside for 10 minutes. Drain, reserving the marinade.

2 Heat 1 teaspoon of the oil in a wok or frying pan and cook the garlic for a few seconds. Add the Quorn or tempeh and stir-fry for 2–3 minutes.

Then transfer to a plate and set aside.
3 Heat the remaining oil in the wok or frying pan and stir-fry the onion wedges for 3–4 minutes, until softened and tinged with brown. Add the fried tofu and chile, stir-fry briefly and then add the noodles. Stir-fry for

4–5 minutes.
4 Stir in the bean sprouts, Chinese chives and most of the ground peanuts, reserving a little for the garnish. Stir well, then add the Quorn or tempeh, the dark soy sauce and the reserved marinade. Continue cooking

for another 1–2 minutes.

5 When hot, spoon onto a serving plate and garnish with the remaining ground peanuts and cilantro.

COOK'S TIP: Quorn makes this a vegetarian meal; however, thinly sliced pork or chicken could be used instead. Stir-fry it initially for 4–5 minutes.

Capellini with Arugula

A light but filling pasta dish with the added pepperiness of fresh arugula, the crispness of snowpeas and the crunchiness of pine nuts.

Serves 1

INGREDIENTS
2½ ounces dried capellini or angel
   hair pasta
2 ounces snowpeas
2½ ounces arugula
1 tablespoon pine
   nuts, roasted
2½ teaspoons finely grated
   Parmesan cheese
2½ teaspoons olive oil

1 Cook the capellini or angel hair pasta, following the instructions on the package, until *al dente*.

2 Trim the snowpeas and separate the arugula leaves.

3 As soon as the pasta is cooked, drop in the arugula and snowpeas, then drain immediately.

4 Toss the pasta in a large bowl with the roasted pine nuts, Parmesan and olive oil. Serve immediately.

Tomato & Fennel Pizza

This pizza relies on the winning combination of tomatoes, fennel and Parmesan. The fennel adds both a crisp texture and a distinctive flavor.

Serves 1

INGREDIENTS
½ small fennel bulb
4½ teaspoons olive oil
1 ready-made pizza crust,
   8–10 inches diameter
1 cup ready-made
   tomato sauce
1 tablespoon chopped fresh
   flat-leaf parsley
¼ cup grated
   mozzarella cheese
⅓ cup grated
   Parmesan cheese
salt and freshly ground
   black pepper

1 Preheat the oven to 425°F. Trim and slice the fennel lengthwise. Remove the core and slice the remaining fennel thinly.

2 Heat 2 teaspoons of the olive oil in a frying pan and sauté the fennel for 4–5 minutes, until just tender. Season.

3 Brush the pizza crust with the remaining oil and spread on the tomato sauce. Spoon the fennel on top and sprinkle on the flat-leaf parsley.

4 Combine the mozzarella and Parmesan and sprinkle on top. Bake for 15 minutes, until crisp and golden. Serve immediately.

Cooked Vegetable Gado–Gado

This tasty Indonesian dish of mixed vegetables, tofu and hard–boiled egg makes a filling supper. Omit the shrimp crackers for vegetarians.

Serves 1

INGREDIENTS
3 ounces mixed cabbage, spinach and bean
    sprouts, rinsed and shredded
1-inch piece of cucumber cut in wedges,
    salted and set aside for 15 minutes
1 egg, hard-boiled and shelled
1 ounce tofu
oil, for frying
2–3 shrimp crackers (optional)
2 ounces waxy potatoes, cooked
    and diced
lemon juice
deep-fried onions, to garnish (optional)

FOR THE PEANUT SAUCE
1 fresh red chile, seeded and ground
⅔ cup coconut milk
6 ounces crunchy peanut butter
1½ teaspoons dark soy sauce or
    dark brown sugar
4½ teaspoons lemon juice
coarsely crushed peanuts
salt

1 First, make the peanut sauce. Put the chile, coconut milk and peanut butter in a pan and heat gently, stirring until smooth. Simmer gently until thickened, then stir in the soy sauce or sugar and lemon juice. Season with salt to taste, pour into a bowl and stir in a few crushed peanuts. Set aside.

2 Bring a large pan of salted water to a boil. Plunge one type of raw vegetable at a time, except the cucumber, into the pan for just a few seconds to blanch. Lift out with a slotted spoon and run under very cold water. Drain thoroughly.

3 Rinse the cucumber pieces and drain them well. Cut the egg in quarters. Cut the tofu into cubes.

4 Fry the tofu in hot oil in a wok until crisp on both sides. Lift out and drain on paper towels.

5 Add more oil to the pan and then deep-fry the shrimp crackers, if using. Drain on paper towels.

COOK'S TIP: Any leftover peanut sauce can be served with grilled chicken to make chicken saté.

6 Arrange all the cooked vegetables, including the potatoes, on a plate, with the cucumber, hard-boiled egg and tofu. Sprinkle with the lemon juice and sprinkle on the fried onions, if using. Serve with the peanut sauce and shrimp crackers, if using.

53

Cracked Wheat Salad

Subtle and unusual flavors are combined in this delicious salad.

Serves 1

INGREDIENTS
5 tablespoons vegetable stock
¼ cinnamon stick
pinch of ground cumin
pinch of ground cloves
pinch of salt
¼ cup cracked wheat
6 snowpeas, trimmed
½ small red and ½ small yellow bell pepper,
    roasted, peeled, seeded and diced
1 small plum tomato, peeled,
    seeded and diced
1 small shallot, finely sliced
2 black olives, pitted and cut into quarters
1½ teaspoons each shredded fresh basil,
    mint and parsley
1½ teaspoons chopped walnuts
1½ teaspoons balsamic vinegar
2 tablespoons extra virgin olive oil
freshly ground black pepper
onion rings, to garnish

1 Put the stock, spices and salt into a saucepan, bring to a boil and cook for 1 minute.

2 Place the cracked wheat in a bowl, pour in the stock and let stand for 30 minutes.

3 In another bowl, combine the snowpeas, peppers, tomato, shallot, olives, herbs and walnuts. Add the vinegar, olive oil and a little black pepper and stir thoroughly to mix.

COOK'S TIP: To roast the peppers, cut in half and place skin-side up on a baking sheet. Place in an oven preheated to 425°F and roast for 20 minutes. Place in a plastic bag for 10 minutes. The skin will then be easily removed.

VARIATION: This salad lends itself to many variations. You could use green beans instead of snowpeas and substitute sun-dried tomatoes for the fresh ones. Other nuts, such as almonds would also be delicious.

4 Strain the cracked wheat of any liquid and discard the cinnamon stick. Transfer to a plate, stir in the fresh vegetable mixture and serve, garnished with onion rings.

Plum, Rum & Raisin Brûlée

Crack through the caramel to find the juicy plums and smooth creamy center of this dessert.

Serves 1

INGREDIENTS
1 tablespoon raisins
2 teaspoons dark rum
3 ounces medium plums
1 tablespoon orange juice
1 teaspoon honey
¼ cup cream cheese
2 tablespoons sugar

2 Quarter the plums and remove their pits. Put into a heavy saucepan, together with the orange juice and honey. Simmer gently for 5 minutes or until soft. Stir in the soaked raisins. Reserve 1 teaspoon of the juice, then transfer the remainder with the plums and raisins into a ⅔-cup ramekin.

1 Put the raisins into a small bowl and sprinkle on the rum. Let soak for 5 minutes.

VARIATION: Simmer a large apple with 1 ounce sugar. Purée, then beat into 1 tablespoon butter. Add a dash of Calvados and chill before finishing as in Step 4.

3 Blend the cream cheese with the reserved plum juice. Spoon onto the plums and raisins and chill in the refrigerator for 1 hour.

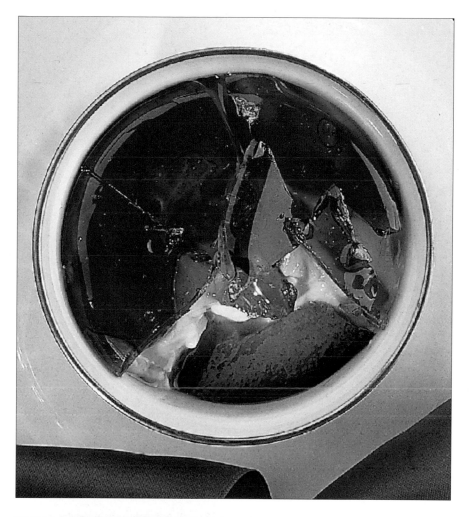

4 Put the sugar into a heavy saucepan with 1 tablespoon cold water. Heat gently, stirring, until the sugar has dissolved. Boil for 10 minutes or until it turns golden brown. Cool for 2 minutes, then carefully pour in the ramekin. Cool and serve.

Fruit Fondue with Hazelnut Dip

Fresh fruit is tasty, easy and good for you, but can become boring. Liven it up with this creamy dip.

Serves 1

INGREDIENTS
selection of fresh fruits for dipping,
    such as satsuma, kiwi fruit,
    grapes, strawberries and cape gooseberries
2 tablespoons cream cheese
5 tablespoons plain yogurt
½ teaspoon vanilla extract
½ teaspoon sugar
2 tablespoons chopped hazelnuts

1 First, prepare the fruits. Peel and segment the satsuma. Then peel the kiwi fruit and cut into wedges. Wash the grapes and strawberries. Peel back the papery casing on the cape gooseberries.

2 Beat the cream cheese with the yogurt, vanilla and sugar in a bowl. Stir in half the hazelnuts. Spoon into a small bowl and sprinkle on the remaining hazelnuts. Arrange the prepared fruits around the dip and serve immediately.

Right: Yogurt Sundae with Passion Fruit Coulis (top); Fruit Fondue with Hazelnut Dip

Yogurt Sundae with Passion Fruit Coulis

Give yourself a treat with all the flavor, but none of the bother, of homemade ice cream.

Serves 1

INGREDIENTS
3 ounces strawberries, hulled and halved
1 small passion fruit, halved
½ teaspoon confectioners' sugar (optional)
1 small ripe peach, pitted and chopped
2 scoops vanilla or strawberry frozen yogurt

1 Purée half the strawberries. Scoop out the passion fruit pulp and add it to the coulis. Sweeten, if necessary.

2 Spoon half the remaining strawberries and half the chopped peach into a sundae glass. Top with a scoop of frozen yogurt. Add another layer of fruit, saving a few pieces for decoration, and another scoop of yogurt. Pour on the coulis and top with the remaining pieces of fruit.

Banana with Caribbean Coffee Sauce

This melt-in-your-mouth dessert has a magical flavor created by setting light to the rum.

Serves 1

INGREDIENTS
1 large banana
1 tablespoon butter
1 tablespoon dark brown sugar
1 tablespoon strong brewed coffee
1 tablespoon dark rum
vanilla ice cream, to serve

1 Peel the banana and cut in half lengthwise. Melt the butter in a large frying pan over medium heat. Add the banana and cook for 3 minutes, turning halfway through cooking time.

2 Sprinkle the sugar on the banana, then add the coffee. Continue cooking, stirring occasionally, for 2–3 minutes or until the banana is tender.

3 Pour the rum into the pan and bring to a boil. With a long match or taper and tilting the pan, ignite the rum. As soon as the flames subside, serve the banana immediately with vanilla ice cream.

Right: Banana with Caribbean Coffee Sauce (top); Nectarine with Coffee Mascarpone

Nectarine with Coffee Mascarpone

This simple dessert is perfect for nectarines that are still slightly hard and underripe.

Serves 1

INGREDIENTS
2 tablespoons Mascarpone cheese
2 teaspoons cold very strong
   brewed coffee
1 nectarine
1 teaspoon melted butter
2 teaspoons honey
pinch of ground all-spice
1 tablespoon slivered Brazil nuts

1 Beat the Mascarpone to soften, then mix in the coffee. Cover with plastic wrap and chill for 20 minutes.

2 Cut the nectarine in half and remove the pit. Mix the butter, 1 teaspoon of the honey and spice. Brush the cut surfaces with the butter.

3 Place the nectarine in an aluminum foil-lined broiler pan. Cook under a hot broiler for 2–3 minutes. Add the Brazil nuts to the broiler pan for the last minute of cooking. Put a spoonful of the cheese mixture in the center of each nectarine half. Drizzle with the remaining honey and sprinkle with the toasted Brazil nuts before serving.

Apple Crêpes

These crêpes are filled with cinnamon-spiced caramelized apples.

Serves 1

INGREDIENTS
½ cup all-purpose flour
pinch of salt
1 egg, beaten
5 tablespoons milk
¼ cup water
1 tablespoon butter, melted
sunflower oil, for frying
cinnamon sugar or confectioners' sugar and
    lemon wedges, to serve (optional)

FOR THE FILLING
1½ tablespoons butter
8 ounces apples, cored, peeled
    and sliced
2 teaspoons sugar
¼ teaspoon ground cinnamon

1 Melt the butter for the filling in a heavy frying pan. When the foam subsides, add the apples, sugar and cinnamon. Cook, stirring occasionally, for 8–10 minutes, until the apples are soft and golden brown. Set aside and keep warm.

2 Sift the flour and salt into a mixing bowl and make a well in the middle. Add the egg and gradually mix in the flour from the sides.

3 Slowly add the combined milk and water, beating until smooth. Stir in the melted butter.

4 Heat 2 teaspoons oil in a crêpe or small frying pan. Pour in about 2 tablespoons of the batter, tilting the pan to coat the bottom evenly.

5 Cook the crêpe until the underside is golden brown, then turn over and cook the other side. Slide onto a warm plate, cover with aluminum foil and set the plate over a pan of simmering water to keep warm. Repeat with the remaining batter mixture, until it is all used up (see Cook's Tip).

6 Divide the apple filling between two crêpes and roll them up. Sprinkle with cinnamon or confectioners' sugar, if desired. Serve with lemon wedges.

COOK'S TIP: This is the smallest convenient amount of crêpe batter, but will be more than is required for one serving. Cook crêpes until all the batter is used up and stack them, interleaved with waxed paper. When cold, wrap the uneaten crêpes in a plastic freezer bag and freeze for up to three months. They can be used individually, will thaw in just a few moments and may be filled or topped with either a savory or sweet filling.

This edition published by Southwater

Distributed in the UK by
The Manning Partnership, 251-253 London Road East,
Batheaston, Bath BA1 7RL, UK
tel. (0044) 01225 852 727 fax. (0044) 01225 852 852

Distributed in Australia by
Sandstone Publishing, Unit 1, 360 Norton Street,
Leichhardt, New South Wales 2040, Australia
tel. (0061) 2 9560 7888 fax. (0061) 2 9560 7488

Distributed in New Zealand by
Five Mile Press NZ, PO Box 33-1071,
Takapuna, Auckland 9, New Zealand
tel. (0064) 9 4444 144 fax. (0064) 9 4444 518

Publisher: Joanna Lorenz
Editor: Valerie Ferguson
Series Designer: Bobbie Colgate Stone
Designer: Andrew Heath
Editorial Reader: Penelope Goodare
Production Controller: Joanna King

Recipes contributed by: Catherine Atkinson,
Carla Capalbo, Lesley Chamberlain,
Maxine Clarke, Carole Clements, Trisha Davies,
Roz Denny, Patrizia Diemling, Matthew Drennan,
Sarah Edmonds, Joanna Farrow, Christine France,
Shirley Gill, Nicola Graimes, Deh-Ta Hsuing,
Shehzad Husain, Christine Ingram, Judy Jackson,
Sallie Morris, Annie Nichols, Maggie Pannell,
Anne Sheasby, Liz Trigg, Hilaire Walden,
Laura Washburn, Steven Wheeler,
Elizabeth Wolf-Cohen.

Photography: Karl Adamson, Edward Allwright,
Steve Baxter, Louise Dove, Mickie Dowie,
James Duncan, Ian Garlick, Michelle Garrett,
Amanda Heywood, Ferguson Hill,
Janine Hosegood, David Jordan, Don Last,
William Lingwood, Patrick McLeavey,
Thomas Odulate.

A CIP catalogue record for this book
is available from the British Library

1 3 5 7 9 10 8 6 4 2

Printed and bound in Singapore